ROCK HOUSE KIDS

GUITAR FOR KIDS

Written & Method By:
John McCarthy

Adapted By: Steve Gorenberg/Jimmy Rutkowski
Supervising Editor: John McCarthy
Music Transcribing & Engraving: Steve Gorenberg/Jimmy Rutkowski
Production Manager: John McCarthy
Layout, Graphics & Design: Steve Gorenberg/Jimmy Rutkowski
Photography: Scott Sawala, Paul Enea, Kathy Kielar
Copy Editor: Cathy McCarthy

Cover Art Direction & Design: Jimmy Rutkowski

HL149901
ISBN: 978-1-4950-3515-9
Produced by John McCarthy

Table of Contents

Welcome to The Rock House Method® system of learning. You are joining millions of aspiring musicians around the world who use our easy-to-understand methods for learning to play music.

Unlike conventional learning programs, The Rock House Method® program is a three-part teaching system that employs downloadable video and audio along with this book to give you a variety of sources to assure a complete learning experience. The downloadable video matches the curriculum exactly, providing you with a live instructor for visual reference. You can pause, rewind, or fast forward any lesson. In addition, you will get free membership to our 24/7 online lesson support site, the website contains valuable bonus lessons, quizzes and additional rhythms and exercises. The audio backing tracks that are used throughout this program can be downloaded and used on any device you choose.

About The Author

John McCarthy is the creator of The Rock House Method®, the world's leading musical instruction system. Over his 25+ year career, he has produced and/or appeared in more than 100 instructional products. Millions of people around the world have learned to play music using John's easy to follow, accelerated program.

John is a virtuoso guitarist who has worked with some of the industry's most legendary musicians. He has the ability to break down, teach and communicate music in a manner that motivates and inspires others to achieve their dreams of playing an instrument.

For more information on John, his music and his instructional products visit www.rockhousemethod.com.

Using the Lesson Support Site

Every Rock House product offers FREE membership to our interactive Lesson Support site. <u>**Use the included member number found on the last page of this book**</u> to register at www.rockhousemethod.com. Once registered, you will use this fully interactive site along with your product to enhance your learning experience, expand your knowledge, link with instructors, and connect with a community of people around the world who are learning to play music using **The Rock House Method®**. There are sections that directly correspond to this product within the **Additional Information** and **Backing Tracks** sections. There are also a variety of other tools you can utilize such as **Ask The Teacher, Quizzes, Reference Material, Definitions, Forums, Live Chats, Guitar Professor** and much more.

Icon Key

When you see an icon in the book, visit the member section of www.rockhousemethod.com for musical backing tracks for you to download and play along with, additional information and other learning utilities.

backing track

additional information

metronome

tablature

tuner

So Easy Quick Tips

Look for quick tips throughout the book, designed to reinforce learning and give you additional pointers.

Parts of the Guitar

Acoustic and electric guitars are very similar. They both have the same number of strings and are tuned the same way. Electric guitars need to be plugged into an amplifier in order to be heard; acoustic guitars can be heard without using an amplifier. The photos in this book will use either acoustic or electric guitars, but the techniques shown can be applied to both.

All guitars are made up of three main sections: the body, the neck and the headstock. All of the other parts of the guitar are mounted on these three sections.

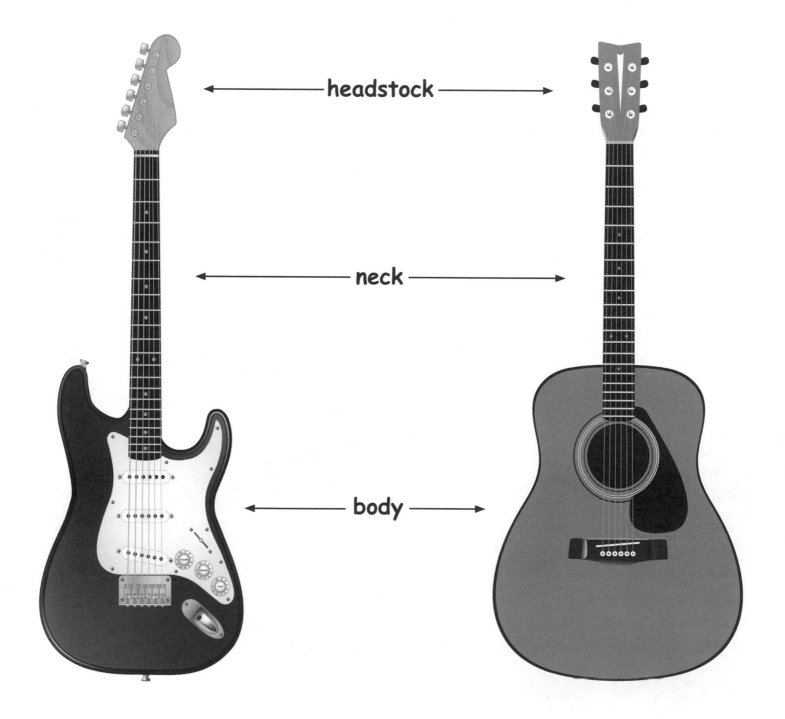

← headstock →

← neck →

← body →

On electric guitars and some acoustic guitars, a guitar cable is plugged into the guitar's input jack. The bridge is the assembly that anchors the strings to the body. Pickups are also mounted to the body and work like little microphones that pick up the sound from the strings. Most electric guitars will also have a pickup selector switch and volume and tone knobs. A guitar strap can be attached to the strap buttons to play the guitar standing up.

The metal bars that go across the neck are called frets. The dots between certain frets are called position markers and help you to know where your hand is on the neck while playing. At the end of the neck is the nut which guides the strings onto the headstock and keeps them in place. On the headstock, the strings are wound around the tuning posts, and the tuners (also called machine heads) are used to tune the strings.

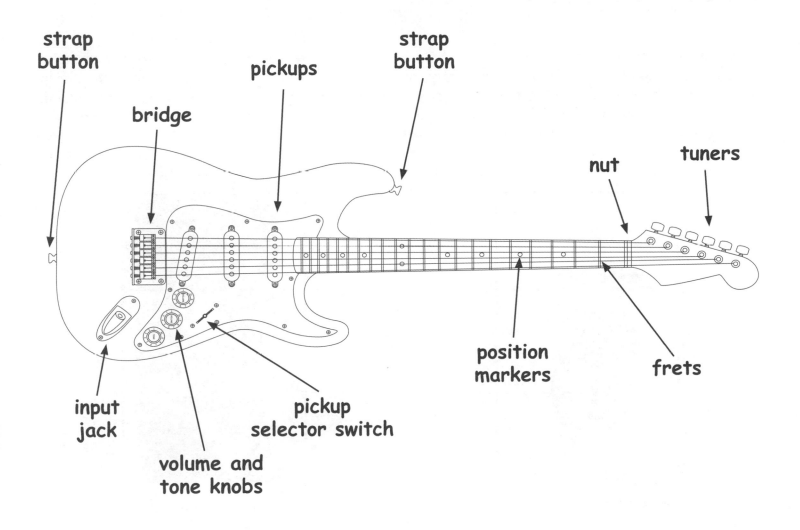

Acoustic guitars have a hollow body with a sound hole (the large round opening under the strings). The guitar's body and sound hole amplify the strings so you can hear them. Some acoustic guitars also have pickups and can be played with or without using an amp.

Holding the Guitar & Pick

Throughout this book, we will refer to the picking hand as your right hand, and the hand fretting the notes as your left hand. If you are left handed and playing a left handed guitar, just make the necessary adjustments as you follow along (read "right hand" to mean your left hand and vice versa).

Holding the Guitar

The photos below show the proper way to hold a guitar. Rest the body of the guitar on your right leg when sitting. When standing, attach a guitar strap to the strap buttons and wear the strap over your left shoulder. Locate the input jack on your guitar. Before you plug in, turn the volume down on the guitar; the amplifier should be off. Plug the cord into the guitar and the amplifier, then turn the amp on and slowly bring up the volume.

Rest the guitar on your right leg when seated.

When standing, the guitar strap goes over your left shoulder.

Attach one end of the guitar strap to the top of the body.

Attach the other end of the strap to the end to the body.

Holding the Pick

Center the pick on the index finger of your right hand.

Bring your thumb down on top of the pick. Pinch your thumb and finger together and leave just the tip of the pick showing.

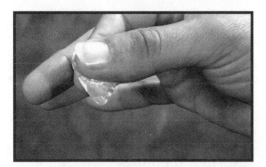

Leave your hand open and your other fingers relaxed (don't make a fist). Your thumb and finger should be placed in the center of the pick, grasping it firmly to give you good control.

Place your right arm on the very top of the guitar and let it drape down almost parallel to the bridge.

Keep your wrist straight and your hand relaxed. The strumming motion should come from your elbow. Strum lightly with just the tip of the pick in a light, smooth motion.

Left Hand Position

Hold your left hand out in front of you with your wrist straight and your fingers curled inward.

Keeping your fingers curled, just naturally bring your hand back to the next of the guitar.

Place the first joint of your thumb against the back of the neck. Try not to bend or contort your wrist; only the tips of your fingers should touch the strings.

Keep Your Hands Loose and Relaxed

Only the first part of your thumb should be touching the back of the neck; don't grab the neck like a baseball bat. Grasp the pick firmly between your thumb and index finger and keep the rest of your right hand relaxed.

Tuning

Each of the six strings on a guitar is tuned to and named after a different note (or pitch). The thinnest or 1st string is referred to as the highest string because it is the highest sounding string. The thickest or 6th string is referred to as the lowest string because it is the lowest sounding string. Memorize the names of the open strings. These notes form the basis for finding any other notes on the guitar.

Names of the Open Strings

6th string	5th string	4th string	3rd string	2nd string	1st string
E	A	D	G	B	E

**6th string (thickest)
lowest sounding string**

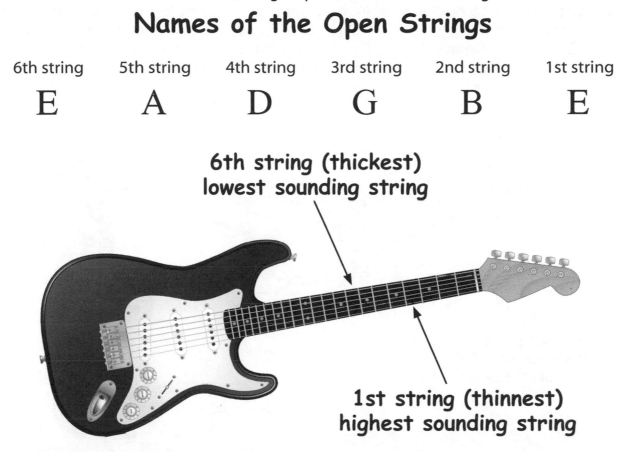

**1st string (thinnest)
highest sounding string**

Tune your guitar using the machine heads on the headstock. Turn the machine heads a little bit at a time while plucking the string and listening to the change in pitch. Tighten the string to raise the pitch. Loosen the string to lower the pitch. Be careful not to accidentally break a string by tightening it too much or too quickly.

The easiest way to tune a guitar is to use an electronic tuner. You can download the free online tuner from www.rockhousemethod.com.

Chord Chart Explanation

A chord is a group of notes played together. A chord chart (also called a chord frame or a chord diagram) is a graph of part of the fretboard showing you which notes to play. The lines going up and down are the strings; the lines going across are the frets.

The solid black dots on the graph are fretted notes and show you where your fingers should go. Each of these dots will have a number directly below it, underneath the diagram. These numbers show you which left hand finger to fret the note with (1 = index, 2 = middle, 3 = ring, 4 = pinky). The 0s at the bottom of the chart show which strings are played open (strummed with no left hand fingers touching them). The strings with Xs below them are not played or strummed.

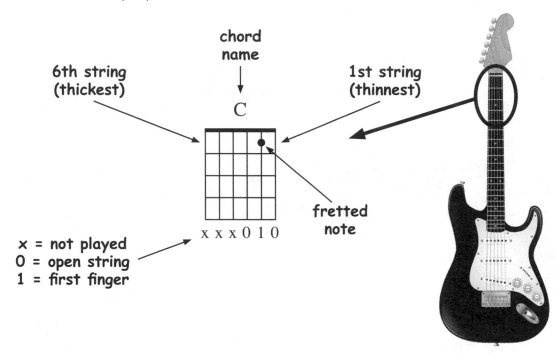

Your First Chords

On the following page are your first three chords: C, G and E. Each chord is shown using a chord chart followed by two photos showing what your hand should look like from the front and side. These are all major chords. Major chords in this book are written using a capital letter by itself.

Remember to keep your thumb anchored against the back of the neck and press down the notes with just your fingertips. Place your fingertip just to the left of (behind) the fret, pressing the string inward toward the neck.

Strum each chord downward towards the floor. The lowest (thickest) three strings in each chord are not played; only strum the highest (thinnest) three strings. Be careful not to let your finger accidentally touch any part of the other strings or they won't ring out. Strum the chords lightly and gently for now until you're comfortable with the strumming motion.

C

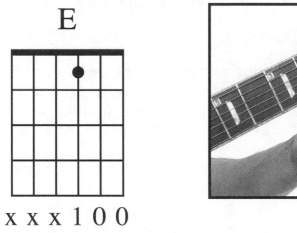

x x x 0 1 0

E

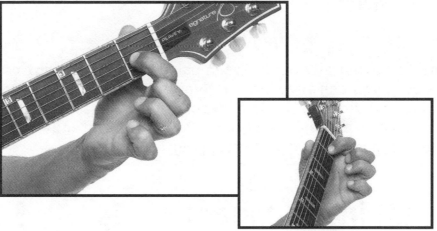

x x x 1 0 0

G

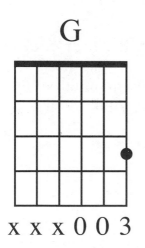

x x x 0 0 3

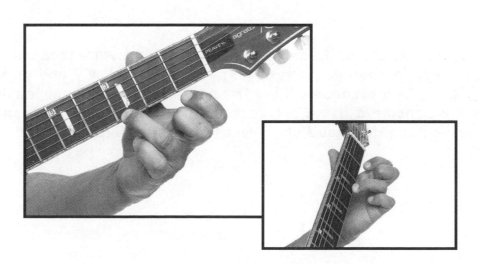

Open String Picking Pattern

In addition to strumming full chords, you can also pick the guitar strings one at a time in a pattern. There are two different ways to pick a string: down or up. The symbols below are used to indicate a downpick or an uppick.

⊓ **downpick - pick down towards the floor**

V **uppick - pick up towards the ceiling**

Learn the following picking pattern using all open strings at first. Once you've got the pattern down, you can try using it to pick out the chords from the previous lesson. Pick each string individually in the order shown; use a down-up-down-up picking motion (called alternate picking). Pick each string in a steady, continuous rhythm, then keep repeating the pattern without stopping.

string number:	3	1	2	1
picking direction:	⊓	V	⊓	V

This is a good exercise to play with a metronome. A metronome is a device that clicks in time at a speed that you can adjust. Start out slowly and pick each string along with the click of the metronome. Play the pattern for five minutes daily and gradually speed up the metronome a little bit each day. You can get a metronome at your local music store or you can download one from the Lesson Support Site.

Counting Along With a Beat: The Quarter Note

Musical notes tell you which note to play and how long each note is held for (or rings out). The amount of time each note is played is referred to as the rhythm or timing. When you play along to a metronome, each click of the metronome is equal to one beat.

The musical note or chord that gets one beat is called a quarter note. Quarter notes are usually counted in groups of four. When you hear a drummer or someone else in the band count off, "One, two, three, four," as a cue in the beginning of a song, they are counting quarter notes.

Quarter Note

To better understand how to count quarter notes, download the rock drum beat backing track for this lesson from the Lesson Support Site. In this drum beat, the drummer alternates between the bass drum and snare drum, steadily playing each for one quarter note on the beat. The bass drum is the big, round, low sounding drum. The snare drum is the higher pitched, fuzzy sounding drum that has a bit of a snap to it.

Start out by tapping your foot in time and on the beat to get in touch with your "body clock". Look at the chart below that shows you how to count and where the bass drum and snare drum hits occur. The bass drum is usually on beats one and three, and the snare drum is on beats two and four. Once you've got your body clock in sync with the beat, try playing just the open 6th string (the lowest sounding string) along with the drum beat in quarter notes. Keep your foot tapping along with the beat and pick the string once for each time your foot touches the ground.

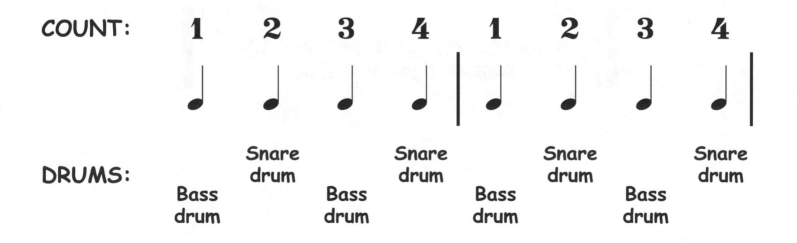

Open String Picking Pattern

Now let's take the G and C small form chords you learned earlier and use them to play your first song rhythm. Starting with the G chord, strum each chord two times. Each strum is held for two beats; the chart below shows you how to count along as you play.

Strum the chords by pivoting from your elbow in a smooth motion. Use all downstrums and keep your arm relaxed. Remember that these are only three note chords and be careful to only strum the 3rd, 2nd and 1st strings. Watch the demonstration on your DVD, then download the bass and drum backing track from the Lesson Support Site and play along.

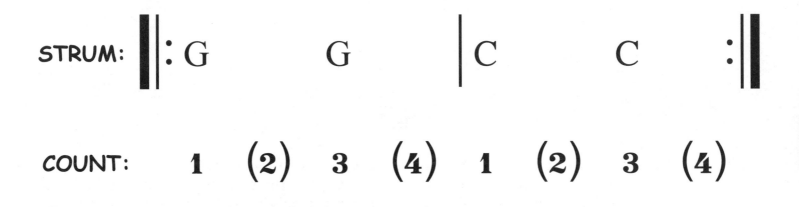

This example also introduces repeat signs. A musical section that's shown in between repeat signs should be played twice.

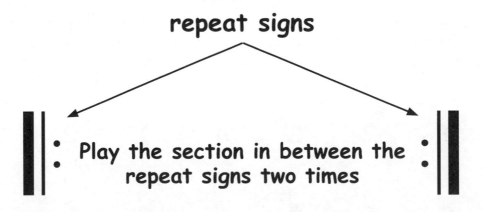

Picking Out the Chords

We can take the song rhythm you just learned and combine it with the 3-1-2-1 picking pattern that you already know. You can play this pattern along with the same bass and drum backing track from the last lesson.

Use the same G and C chords from the last lesson. Instead of strumming, pick out the notes of the chords individually using the picking pattern. Follow the repeat signs and play the pattern twice for each chord. Be sure you're using alternate picking. Start out slowly without the backing track until you're used to applying the pattern along with the chord change.

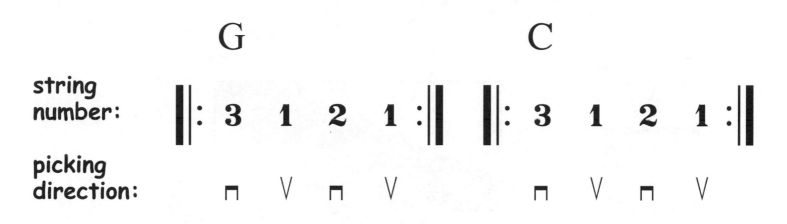

| G | C |

string number: ‖: 3 1 2 1 :‖ ‖: 3 1 2 1 :‖

picking direction: ⊓ V ⊓ V ⊓ V ⊓ V

Don't Get Frustrated!

Don't be discouraged if you can't get something right away. Learning the guitar takes time and practice. Once you've got the basics down, it gets easier. Keep practicing and make sure you've got each lesson mastered before you continue.

Minor Open Chords

Here are your first two minor chords: **A minor and E minor.** The small "m" in a chord name indicates that it is a minor chord. Minor chords have a sad sound, while major chords have a happy or bright sound.

The Am and Em chords below are full open chords and use more than one finger to fret the notes. Study the photos and look at the chord frames carefully to make sure you've got the correct fingers on the right notes. Strum the chords out and let all of the notes ring together. If you hear any muted or dead notes, pick each note of the chord out one at a time and adjust your fingers slightly to get the chord sounding as clean as possible.

Am

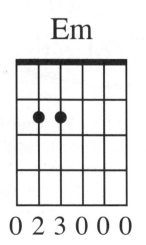

x 0 2 3 1 0

Em

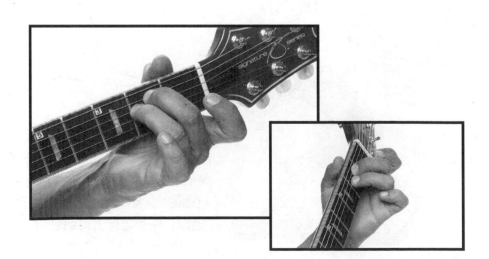

0 2 3 0 0 0

Counting Along With a Beat: Whole Notes & Half Notes

Whole notes receive four beats; half notes receive two beats. When playing whole notes, strum the note or chord and let it ring out for a full four beats. Use the same drum beat backing track that we used to demonstrate quarter notes and play the open 6th string along with it in whole notes. Then use the same note to play half notes along with the beat.

The charts below show you how to play whole notes and half notes and count along with the beat. The numbers in parentheses show which beats the note is held over without striking it again. Learning how to count whole notes, half notes and quarter notes along with a drum beat should give you a solid foundation for rhythm and timing.

WHOLE NOTES:	o				o			
COUNT:	1	(2)	(3)	(4)	1	(2)	(3)	(4)

HALF NOTES:	♩		♩		♩		♩	
COUNT:	1	(2)	3	(4)	1	(2)	3	(4)

Strumming Complete
Song Rhythms

This song rhythm uses the full Am and Em chords. Download the backing track from the website and practice along with the band. Start with the Am chord and downstrum four times, being careful to only strum from the 5th string down. Then switch to the Em chord and strum all six strings. Make sure you are only strumming the correct strings for each chord in a clean, steady motion.

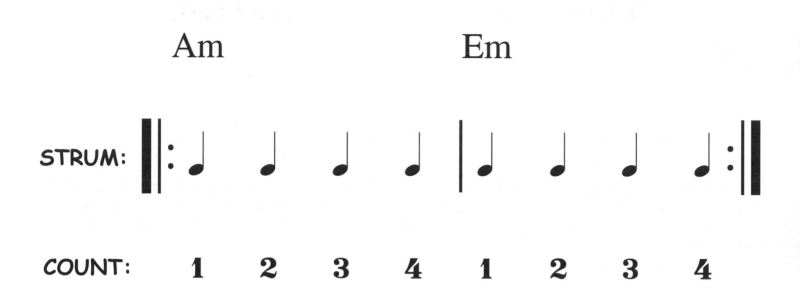

When changing from chord to chord, keep your hand in place on the neck and slightly adjust your fingers to play the next chord. Use the smallest amount of finger movement possible to switch from chord to chord without taking your whole hand off the guitar. If you find it difficult to change chords in time and on the beat, practice just changing from chord to chord without the backing track at first. This will help build finger memory and make your chord changes clean and smooth.

Tablature Explanation

Tablature (or tab) is a number system for reading notes on the neck of a guitar. Most music for guitar is available in tab. The six lines of the tablature staff represent each of the six strings. The top line is the thinnest (highest pitched) string. The bottom line is the thickest (lowest pitched) string. The lines in between are the 2nd through 5th strings. The numbers placed directly on these lines show you the fret number to play the note at. At the bottom, underneath the staff, is a series of numbers. These numbers show you which left hand fingers you should use to fret the notes.

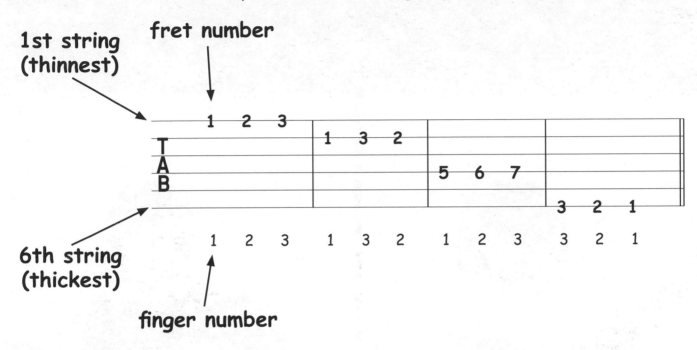

Chords can also be written in tab. If there are several numbers stacked together in a column, those notes should be played or strummed at the same time. Here are the five chords you already know from the previous lessons with the tablature written out underneath each diagram.

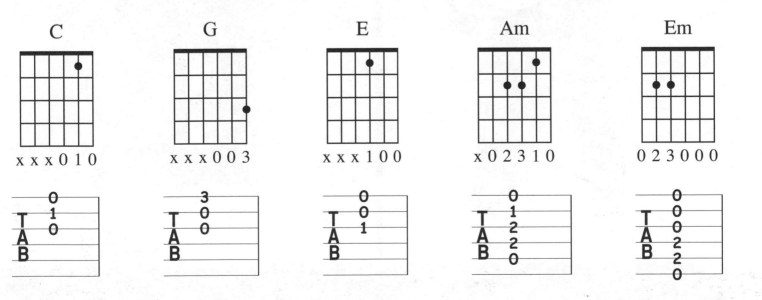

21

Quiz #1

1) The frets are located on which part of the guitar?
A. the body
B. the headstock
C. the neck
D. the strap

2) The pickups are located on which part of the guitar?
A. the body
B. the headstock
C. the neck
D. the bridge

3) The tuners are located on which part of the guitar?
A. the body
B. the headstock
C. the neck
D. the input jack

4) The names of the open strings, from lowest to highest pitched, are:
A. B-E-G-A-D-E
B. A-G-E-B-E-D
C. E-A-D-G-B-E
D. A-B-C-D-E-F

5) Quarter notes are held for
A. one quarter of a beat
B. four beats
C. one beat
D. a quarter of a second

6) A down-up-down-up picking motion is called
A. normal picking
B. up and down picking
C. alternate picking
D. back and forth picking

7) The six lines of the tablature staff represent
A. six different chords
B. the six strings of the guitar
C. the first six frets on the guitar
D. nothing

Answers to the review quiz are located on page 72

Playing a Simple Melody #1

You can also play melodies on the guitar. A melody is a succession of single notes. Our first melody is When the Saints Go Marching In.

The notes are shown below in tab with the left hand finger numbers written out underneath. Watch the demonstration on the DVD and learn each phrase one at a time, repeating and practicing it until you've got it memorized. Take your time; there's a lot of notes to remember. Start out slowly and make sure you're picking the right strings. Listen to the notes as you play them and use your ear to help you along. This melody is easy to recognize, so you'll probably notice right away if you play any wrong notes.

When the Saints Go Marching In

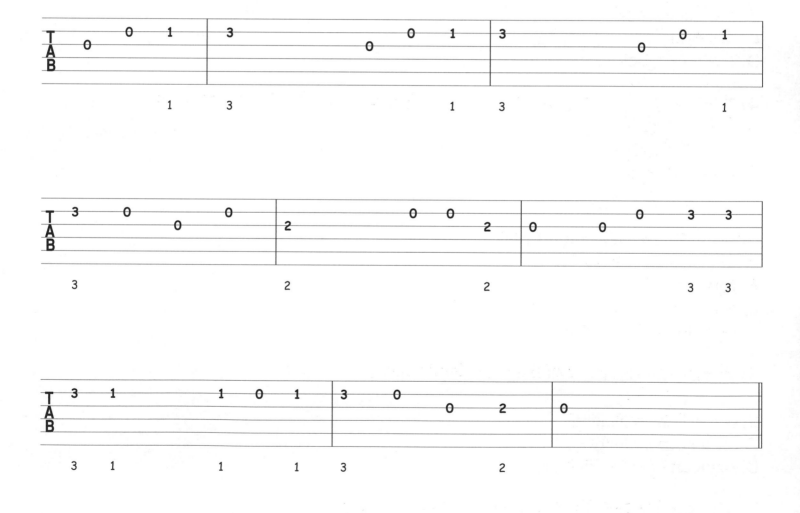

Picking Pattern #2

This is a more complicated picking pattern you can use to pick out the Am and Em full open chords. The order of the strings to pick is 4-1-3-1-2-1. Start out learning the pattern by just using open strings. Be sure to use alternate picking and practice the pattern along with a metronome every day.

string
number: ‖: 4   1   3   1   2   1 :‖

picking
direction: ⊓   V   ⊓   V   ⊓   V

Once you've got the picking pattern, try applying it to the Am and Em chords as shown on the tab staff below. When you can change chords and still keep the picking motion continuous and steady, it will sound like a real song. You can use this pattern to pick out any of the chords in this book and start to write your own original songs.

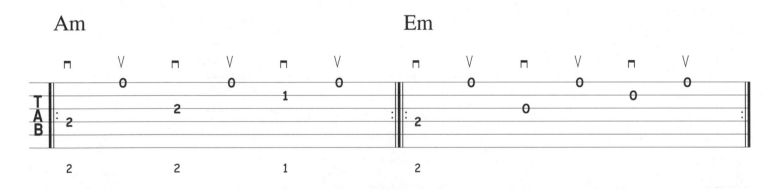

Check Your Tuning!

It's always a good idea to stop and check your tuning. You might be playing the right notes, but it won't sound good if your guitar is out of tune. New strings tend to go out of tune a lot before they get broken in.

Playing a Simple Melody #2

Our second melody is Happy Birthday to You. This is a great song to learn and play for your friends and family. Follow the fingering under the tab staff and practice each phrase until you have it memorized. Once you've got it, try to sing along!

Once you're comfortable reading tablature and playing these melodies, visit the website at www.rockhousemethod.com to get many more songs in tablature.

The B-Day Song

Counting Along With a Beat: Eighth Notes

Eighth notes are played for half a beat, or half the value of a quarter note. Eighth notes can be written individually using a flag or grouped together using beams.

Using the same drum beat that we used to count quarter notes, tap your foot on the beat and count "One and two and three and four and." Your foot should touch the floor on each beat like before. This is called the downbeat. When you say the word "and" in between the beats, your foot should be up in the air. This is called the upbeat. On the backing track, the cymbal that's being played along with the drums is playing in eighth notes.

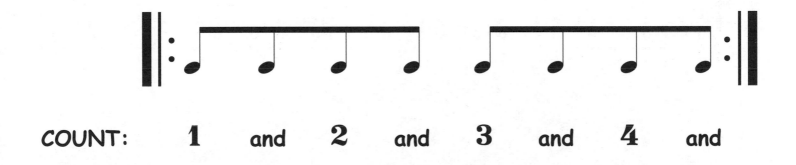

Play eighth notes on the open 6th string along with the beat. Since there are two eighth notes for each beat, you should be playing twice as fast as when you were playing quarter notes. Use alternate picking, count along and keep your foot tapping on the downbeats.

Basic Blues

The following is a basic blues riff in the key of A. This riff is made up of two note chords shown on the tab staff. The chord names above the staff are there as a reference to show you what the basic harmony is while you play along.

This riff should sound very familiar - it's used more than any other blues progression. Plenty of rock and blues classics are played entirely with this one riff repeated over and over. It is made up of twelve measures (or bars) of music called the 12-bar blues, a blues progression consisting of twelve repeated bars of music.

Blues is played with a shuffle feel. Shuffle feel is a much easier concept to understand by hearing it. Listen to the backing track, count along and try to get the shuffle feel in your head. To play eighth notes with a shuffle feel, the second eighth note of each beat should lag a little. Once you've got the blues feel in your head and the riff memorized, play along with the bass and drums and get the blues.

A

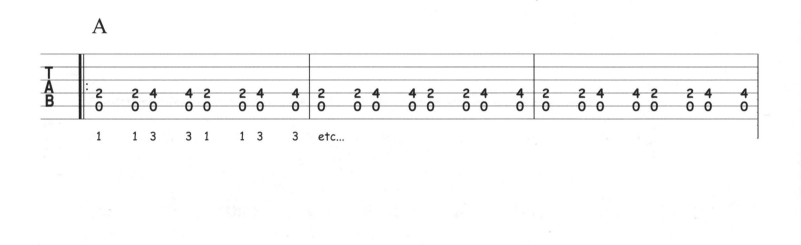

D

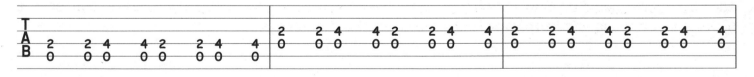

28

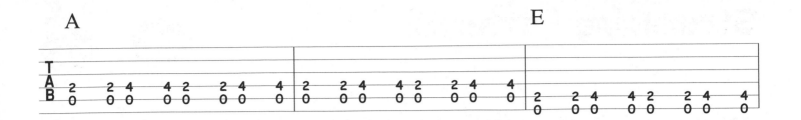

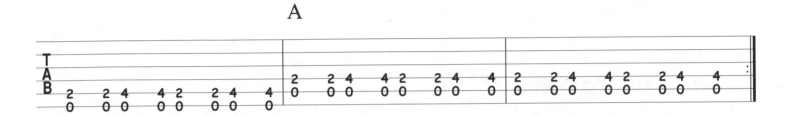

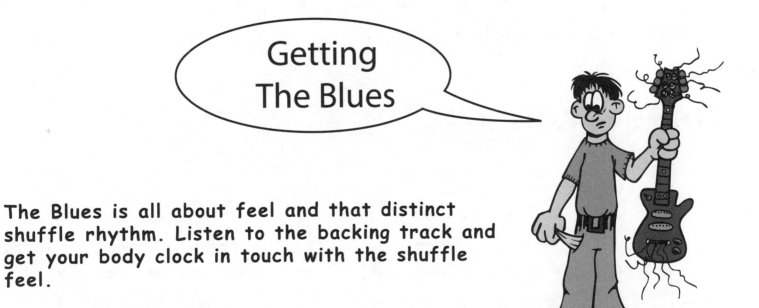

Getting
The Blues

The Blues is all about feel and that distinct
shuffle rhythm. Listen to the backing track and
get your body clock in touch with the shuffle
feel.

Strumming Patterns

Until now, we've played chords using all downstrums. In this lesson we'll show you a few strumming patterns that use upstrumming and downstrumming. The same symbols we used for picking direction are also used to show the strumming direction.

Count out the rhythm as shown under each example and practice changing from chord to chord in time. Play the rhythm slowly at first using the metronome, then play along with the same backing track from the Song Rhythms lesson on page 20.

After you've got these patterns down, visit the Lesson Support Site for more rhythms and strumming patterns.

Strumming Pattern #1

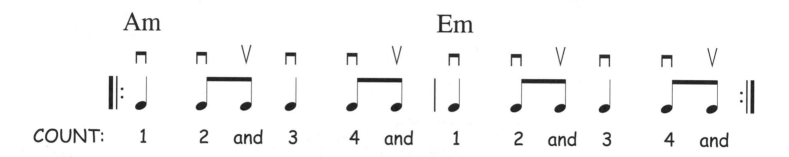

Strumming Pattern #2

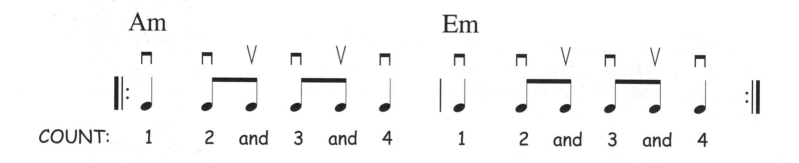

More Chords: Full Open Chords

This section contains a number of full open major chords. The first chord, C major, uses three fingers and is the full version of the small form C chord you learned earlier. Be careful not to let any of your fingers deaden the open strings that need to ring out. Your fingers should push the strings straight down against the neck; don't tilt your fingers and accidentally mute any other strings.

C

x 3 2 0 1 0

The E major chord uses three fingers as well. Notice how similar the fingering is to the Em chord you learned previously; just add your first finger to the 1st fret on the 3rd string and you've got it.

E

0 2 3 1 0 0

In the A major chord diagram, the slur going across the notes means you should barre (pronounced "bar") those notes. A barre is executed by placing one finger flat across more than one string. Pick each note of the chord individually to make sure you're applying enough pressure to all of the strings with your first finger. Notice that the 6th and 1st strings each have an "x" below them on the diagram, indicating these strings are not played (either muted or not strummed). Be carful not to accidentally strike the 1st string when you strum the chord.

A

x 0 1 1 1 x

Practice Changing Chords

Try to make your chord changes smooth so you don't hesitate and go out of time when playing songs. Sometimes one or two of your fingers can stay in the same place when moving from one chord to the next.
Only move the fingers you need to and avoid taking your whole hand off the guitar.

The D major chord is a very popular three finger chord. Practice changing back and forth between the D and A chords and the D and E chords. These are both common chord changes in many different songs and musical styles.

D

x 0 0 1 3 2

The G major chord is played using all four fingers and is the first chord to use your 4th finger. Pick each note out and make sure your fingers aren't deadening any of the other strings.

G

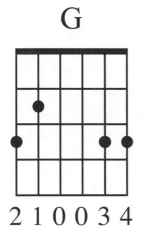

2 1 0 0 3 4

Minor Pentatonic Scales

To play lead guitar you need to learn scales. A scale is a series of single notes and make up the vocabulary you'll use to playing solos. In this lesson, we'll show you the first position of the most popular scale: the A minor pentatonic scale.

The first position is shown here in tab ascending (going up the scale from the lowest to the highest notes) and descending (going back down the scale). Memorize the scale and practice to a metronome using alternate picking until you are comfortable with the scale. Watch the demonstration on your DVD to learn how to mix up the notes into phrases, then mix up the notes yourself to start creating your own melodies and solos.

The A Minor Pentatonic Scale (Ascending)

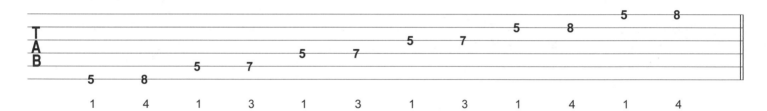

The A Minor Pentatonic Scale (Descending)

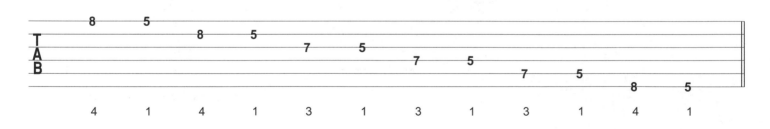

Power Chords

Power chords are simple two note chords that are used in a lot of rock songs. Since they have no open strings, they are moveable chords. When you move a power chord to a different fret, the note name of the chord changes to the note at the new fret.

Power chords are usually played with your first finger either on the sixth or the fifth string. Both forms are shown here at the first fret. The chart at the bottom shows you the names of the chords all the way up the neck to the 12th fret.

F5

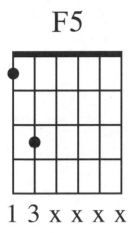

1 3 x x x x

B♭5

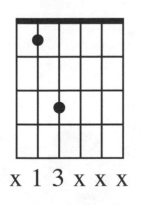

x 1 3 x x x

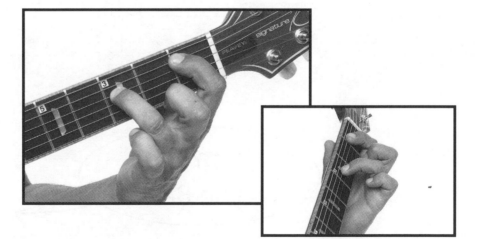

6th string:	E	F	F♯	G	G♯	A	A♯	B	C	C♯	D	D♯	E
	Open	1	2	3	4	5	6	7	8	9	10	11	12
5th string:	A	B♭	B	C	C♯	D	D♯	E	F	F♯	G	G♯	A

Strumming Patterns

Now let's take use power chords from the previous lesson to play a complete rock rhythm. All of the chords in this progression will use the 6th string power chord form. The exercise is shown in tab below and is played using a quarter note rhythm.

For the first chord, play the power chord form at the 5th fret, making it an A5 power chord. Then for the second chord, move your hand to the 3rd fret to play a G5 power chord. For the third chord, bring the chord all the way down to the 1st fret to play the F5 power chord. Then go back up to the G5 power chord at the 3rd fret and repeat the entire progression.

Once youv'e learned the chords, practice along with the bass and drum backing track until you've got it in time and on the beat with the band. When you have it mastered, try to vary the rhythm by playing eighth notes or half notes. Mix up the rhythms and create some new combinations.

You can download all of the backing tracks in this program and make a CD to practice to, letting you jam along with a real drummer and bass player. This will help get you ready to start your own band!

Quiz #2

1) A succession of single notes is called
A. a chord progression
B. rhythm
C. a melody
D. music

2) Blues is played using
A. minor chords
B. a shuffle feel
C. all major chords
D. a metronome

3) Minor chords have
A. five notes
B. two notes
C. a sad sound
D. a happy, bright sound

4) Power chords have
A. five notes
B. two notes
C. a sad sound
D. a happy, bright sound

5) Eighth notes are held for
A. half a beat
B. four beats
C. one beat
D. half a second

6) Fretting more than one note with one finger is called
A. scales
B. a chord
C. a barre

D. alternate fretting
7) Power chords are
A. loud chords
B. open chords
C. moveable chords
D. removeable chords

Answers to the review quiz are located on page 72

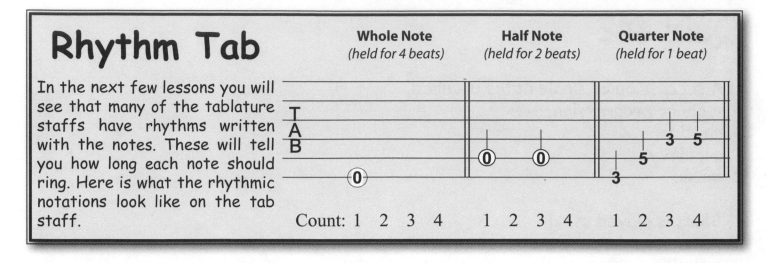

Rockin' the Bells

In this melody you will be playing quarter, half and whole notes. Practice each line separately then put the whole song together. Once you can play the song from beginning to end without stopping, play it along with the full band backing track.

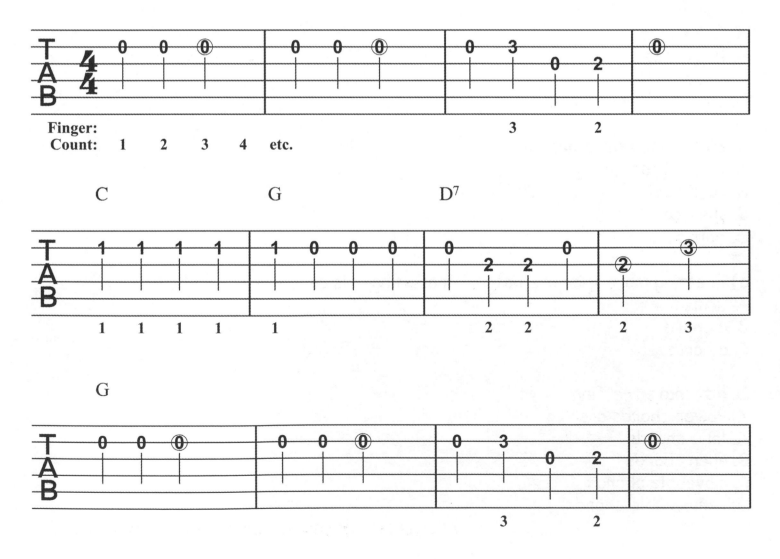

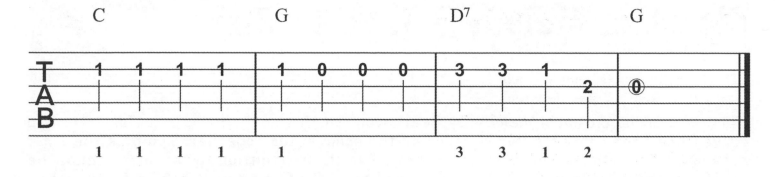

Blues Riff Rhythm

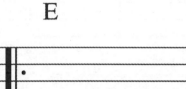

The following is a single note blues riff rhythm. This is a common rhythm so it should sound familiar. Be sure to play this over the bass and drum backing track.

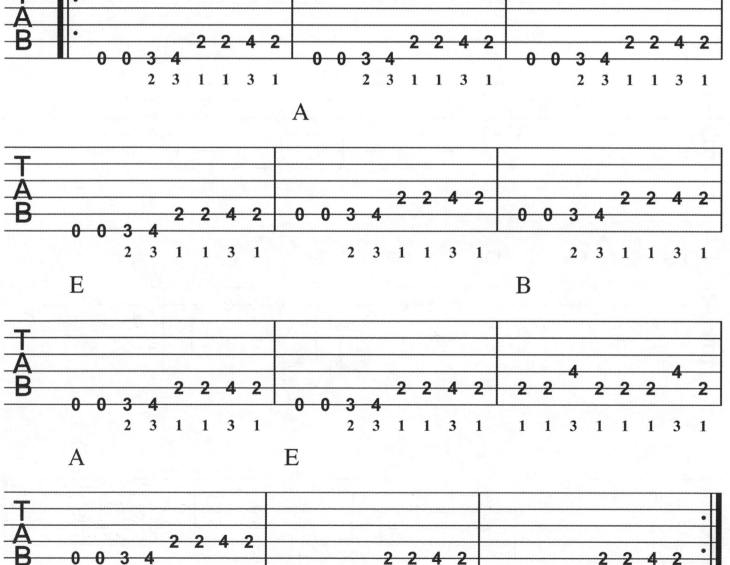

Classical Melody - Ode to Joy

Here is a great classical melody by Beethoven. In this song there is a tie. A tie is a curved line that connects two or more of the same notes together. You pick the first note and let it ring for the duration of both. Pay close attention to the count below the staff for these measures, the next note will be pick on an up beat or the & count. I've included the chords for the song above the staff. Once you have learned the melody, play the rhythm by strumming the chords above the staff along with the melody.

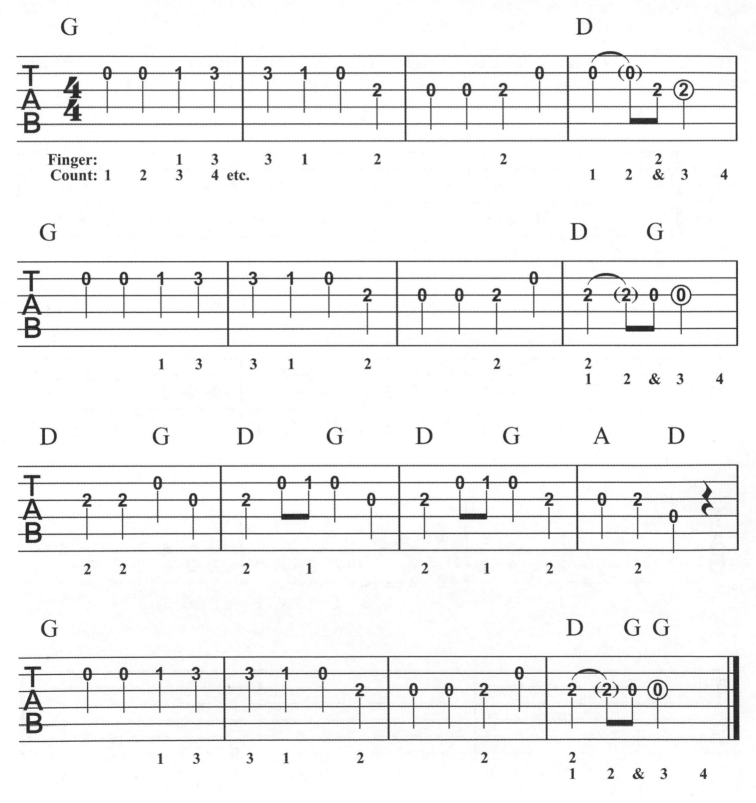

Beats, Rhythm, Timing

Table of Contents

Counting Along with a Beat

In this lesson, you will learn how to count along with a piece of music that contains drums, bass, and guitar. Most music is commonly in 4/4 timing. It's subdivided into four beat sections; therefore, you will count in sections of four like this: 1 – 2 – 3 – 4, 1 – 2 – 3 – 4, 1 – 2 – 3 – 4 and so on.

Pay attention to the drums as you count with the backing track. If you listen closely, the bass drum is hit on beats 1 and 3, while the snare drum is hit on beats 2 and 4.

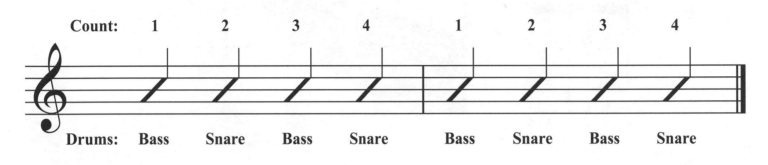

Your Body Clock

I'm sure many times you've had a song playing and you were tapping your foot or bobbing your head to it, that's what I call using your "body clock." In this lesson, you will learn to develop your body clock by tapping your foot along with a drumbeat.

You will tap your foot and count along with the drumbeat that we previously learned. The proper way to do this is to put your heel down on the ground, and pivot your toes up and down to keep the beat. The result will be down, up, down, up while keeping your heel firmly on the ground.

Foot Down   Foot Up

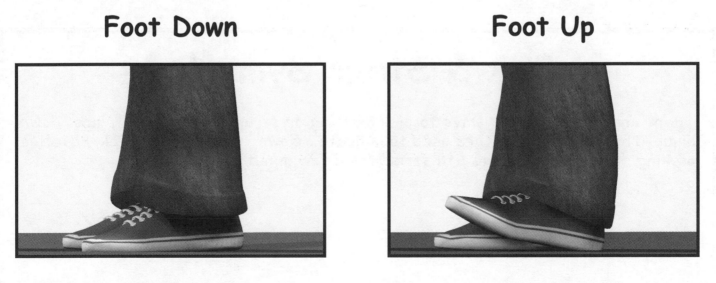

For further practice, I want you to tap your foot along with some of your favorite songs. This will help you get comfortable using your body clock. Remember, keep your heel planted on the ground and your foot constantly going up and down.

Basic Chords

Let's review two of the chords that you will use for many of the playing examples in this program. The two chords are open E and A minor. Minor chords tend to have a sad tonality to them. Study the chord diagrams carefully to make sure you have the correct fingers fretting the notes. Pick each chord one note at a time then give them a big strum.

Em

0 2 3 0 0 0

Am

0 2 3 1 0

X 0 2 3 1 0

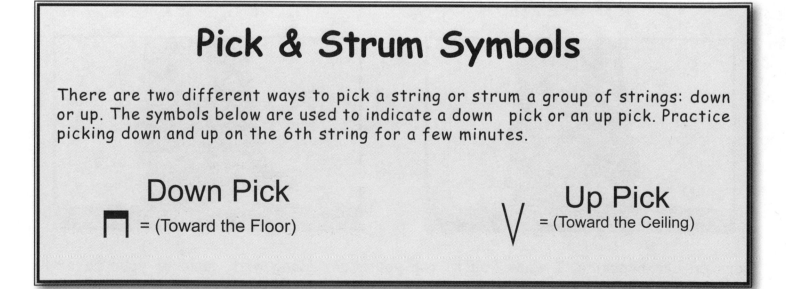

Pick & Strum Symbols

There are two different ways to pick a string or strum a group of strings: down or up. The symbols below are used to indicate a down pick or an up pick. Practice picking down and up on the 6th string for a few minutes.

Down Pick

⊓ = (Toward the Floor)

Up Pick

V = (Toward the Ceiling)

Muting Techniques & Basic Strumming

Strumming is a great way to further develop your body clock. You will not only learn how to strum properly using your inner body clock, but you will also be tapping your foot and counting aloud as you play to further strengthen the concepts you have learned thus far.

Before you begin strumming chords and playing chord progressions, it is important to learn muting. Begin by placing all four fretting fingers on the strings, however; don't press the strings down. Just touch the strings lightly. When you strum downward across the strings, no musical sound should come from your guitar, it should just be a percussive sound. If you press too hard, you will get miscellaneous string noises that you don't want, you only want to hear a muted sound. This is notated in tab as x's.

Now with your strumming arm, pivot from your elbow, holding your pick between your index finger and thumb while keeping your hand open. Do not have your hand in a closed fist, and keep your strumming hand, arm and shoulder loose and relaxed while strumming. Now while muting the strings, keep your strumming arm relaxed and strum down and up across all six strings.

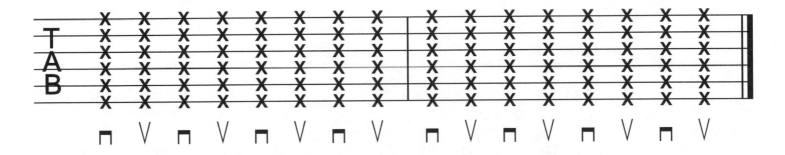

Next you will strum along with the drum beat you worked with earlier. Tap your foot down and up while you strum down and up in sync. So when your foot goes down, you strum down. When your foot goes up, you strum up. Fret the E minor chord and strum down up while tapping your foot.

Em

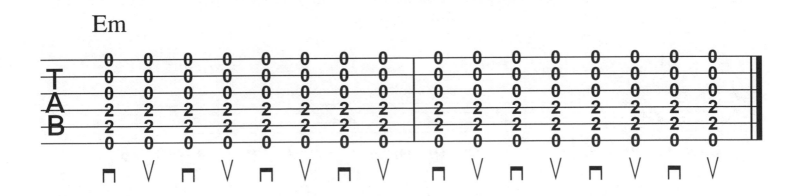

Once you have practiced this several times you should be getting the basic technique of strumming together. Make sure that you feel your inner body clock getting in sync with the rhythm and rhythmic motion of your strumming. Get excited, in the next section you are going to start learning about several different note values that you will start applying to rhythms as well.

Note Values
Whole Notes

◢◢	4	When used in strumming rhythms the whole note will still be hollow with no stem, only the shape will be slightly different as shown here.
Whole Note	**Beats**	

A whole note receives four beats. If you pick a note or strum a chord in whole note timing the sound will ring out for four beats, or four taps of your foot. Fret the E minor open chord, count 1 – 2 – 3 – 4 and strum the chord on every 1 count. Be sure to let the sound ring while you count 2 – 3 – 4.

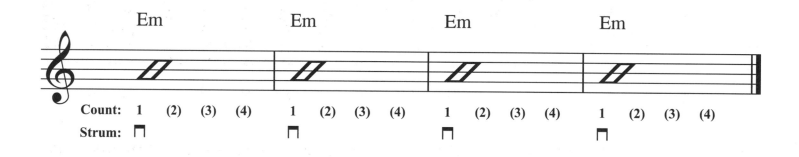

Now play whole notes along with the backing track. Remember each chord will ring for four beats. Strum the E minor once, let it ring for four beats, then strum the A minor chord once, let that ring for four beats. Keep alternating between the two chords for the length of the backing track.

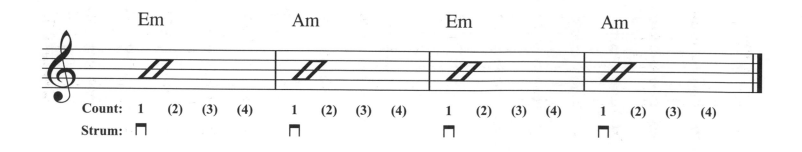

Half Notes

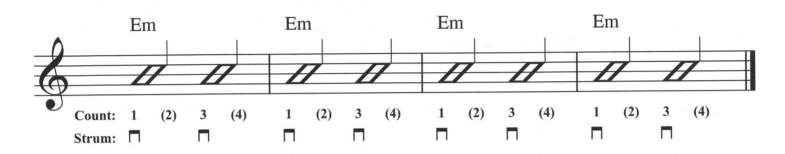

A half note receives two beats. If you pick a note or strum a chord in half note timing the sound will ring out for two beats, or two taps of your foot. Fret the E minor open chord, count 1 – 2 – 3 – 4 and strum the chord on every 1 and 3 count. Be sure to let the sound ring on counts 2 and 4.

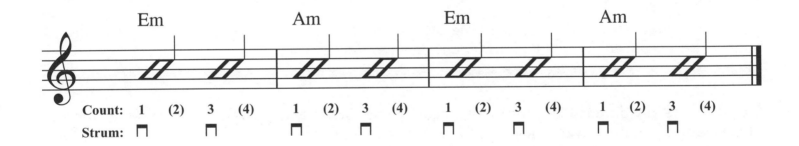

Play the half note exercise with the bass and drum backing track. Strum the E minor chord, in half note timing twice then switch to A minor and play it the same way. Keep repeating the two chords played in half notes with the backing track making sure that you are tapping your foot, counting aloud and keeping your strumming arm and hand relaxed.

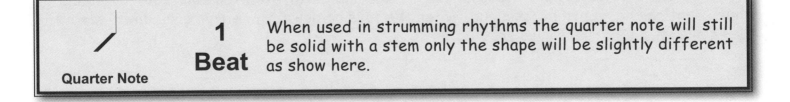

Quarter Notes

A quarter note receives one beat. So every time you tap your foot down, you play a note or a chord. Holding the E minor chord down, strum it while counting 1 – 2 – 3 – 4 strumming once for each count. Every number and every time your foot hits the ground, you're hitting one chord.

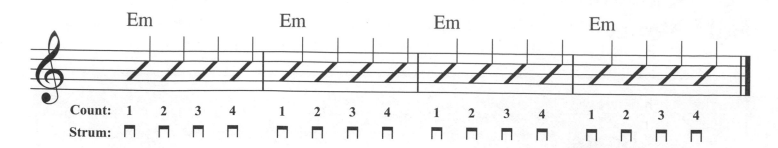

Play the quarter note exercise with the bass and drum backing track. Remember each chord is going to get one beat so every time your foot hits the ground; you're strumming another chord. You are going to play the E minor four times, then the A minor four times repeating the two chords for the length of the backing track.

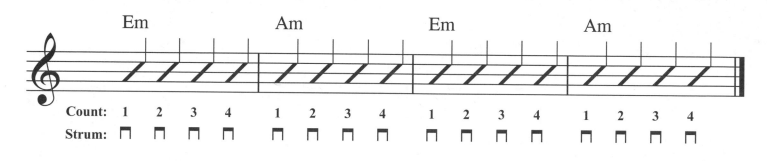

Eighth Notes

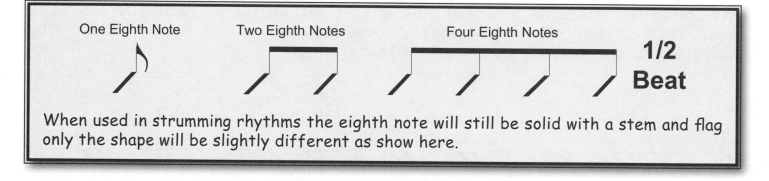

Eighth notes divide each beat into two equal parts. When you played the quarter notes you strummed your guitar every time your foot tapped the floor. With eighth notes you will strum a chord every time your foot taps the ground and also every time your foot goes up. Count the beat number on the down and & on the up as follows: 1 – & – 2 – & – 3 – & – 4 – & – 1 – & – 2 – & – 3 – & – 4 – &. The 1, 2, 3 and 4 counts will be down strums, and the "&'s" will be up strums.

Holding an E minor chord down, count the 1 while strumming downward and when you count the "&" strum the strings upward. Keeping the strums and count even tap your foot down and up while counting the eighth notes aloud. When the toes go down, the strum goes down, when the toes come up, the strum comes up.

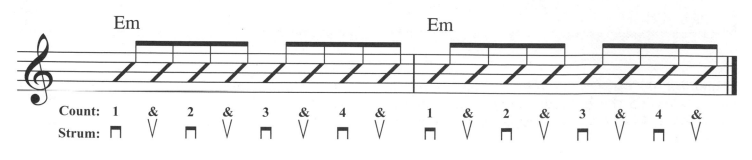

The key to success is to remember the numbers are down and the "&'s" are up strums. By keeping this synchronized properly you will find that the strumming motion of your arm is acting like a "rhythm-keeper" for you, which is an outward visual of your inner body clock, all working properly.

Play the eighth note exercise along with the backing track. Remember to count along as you strum. Your arm should be relaxed and move in a steady even motion.

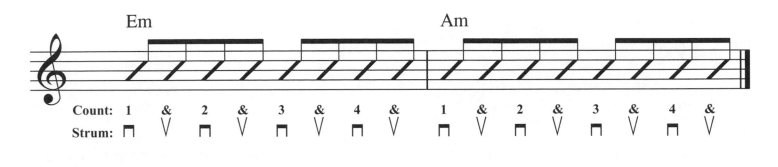

Strum Patterns

Strum Pattern #1

In this lesson you are going to learn how to combine different note values together to create strum patterns. The first strum pattern will combine quarter and eighth notes. The first pattern will be: down, down-up-down, down-up. Pay close attention to the count below the staff to play the pattern in time properly. Also, notice how these different note values add up to four beats in each measure. It is important that your strum patterns add up to the correct number of beats in each measure. A great way to get comfortable with the strumming rhythm is to first just apply it to the E minor chord only. Once you get the feel of the strum, tap your foot and count the notes while you play the strum pattern. Strum the E minor and A minor chords following the staff below:

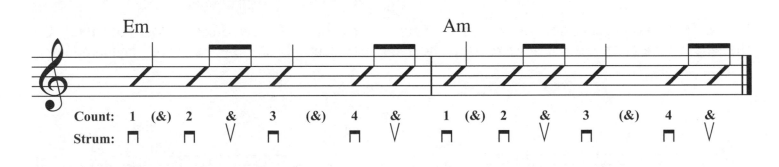

Strum Pattern #2

for each chord. The physical strumming of this pattern is played down, down, down-updown- up. Keep your strumming arm loose and flowing as you strum the pattern. The way you will count this strum pattern is 1 – 2 – 3 – & – 4 – &. The quarter notes are 1 and 2, and 3 – & – 4 – & are the four eighth notes. Practice the strum pattern with the E minor chord only to get familiar with the pattern. Next play the pattern along with the bass and drum-backing track. As you play the pattern count aloud, tap your foot and most importantly, stay relaxed.

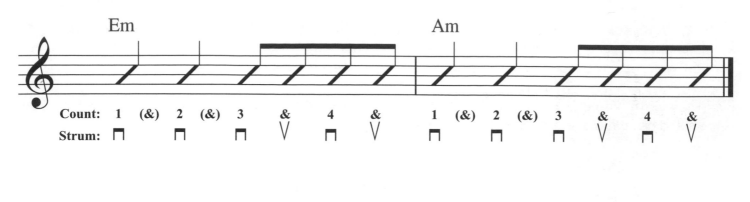

Rests

Rests are a period of silence. For instance, a quarter note rest would receive one beat of silence; whereas a quarter note receives one beat of sound. You will learn about four different types of rests in this section. As you just learned about the quarter note rest, the same principle applies; each of the four rests will have the same beat denomination as the note it corresponds with.

Whole Note Rest

Let's start with a whole note rest. A whole note rest is a little black box that would hang off of the fourth line of a music staff and receives four beats of silence.

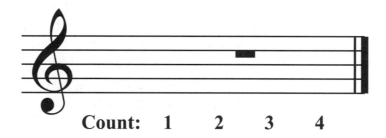

In the following progression you will strum four quarter notes followed by a whole note rest. On the whole note rest you will have to stop the sound and count 1 – 2 – 3 – 4 before playing again.

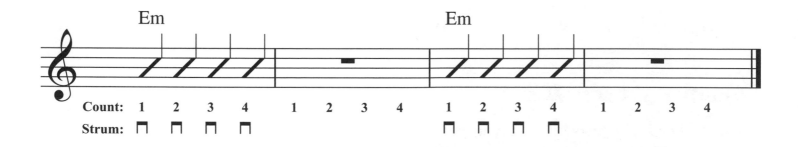

Half Note Rest

A half note rest also looks like a box, but this one sits on top of the third staff line, facing up. An easy way to decipher the half note rest and the whole note rest is that the whole note rest hangs from the line so you can think of it as "heavier" so it is hanging.

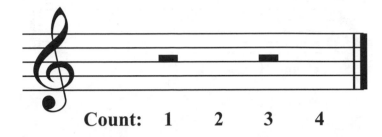

A half note rest will receive two beats of silence, the half note receives two beats of sound. The following progression will have a half note followed by a half rest. You will strum the chord and let it ring for two beats then stop the sound from ringing for two more beats and repeat this for each measure. There will be two beats of sound followed by two beats of silence. These beats of silence could be anywhere in the measure, it doesn't have to just be the last two beats.

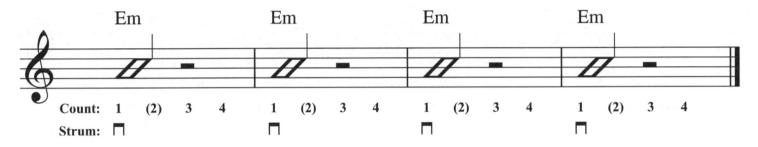

Quarter Note Rest

A quarter note rest looks like a jagged line; it almost looks like a lightning bolt within the notation staff.

A quarter note rest gets one beat of silence and the quarter note gets one beat of sound. The following progression goes as follows, quarter note strum, quarter note rest, quarter note strum, quarter note rest. Play the following progression using the quarter note rests:

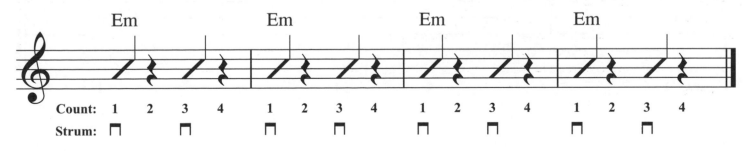

Eighth Note Rest

The last rest to be covered in this program is the eighth note rest. The eighth note rest looks like a seven with a little ball at the end on the top.

These rests could be placed anywhere in the measure, it doesn't have to be on the second part of the beat. Play the following progression that is a series of eighth note strums followed by eighth note rests:

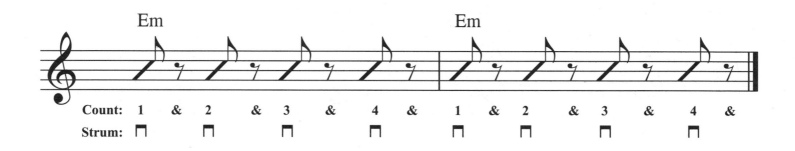

Using Staccato with Quarter Notes

The term Staccato means short and detached. When a note is played staccato there's a period of silence, almost like a rest after each note. The notes are played then deadened immediately.

Staccato is notated in music by putting a dot on top of a note. Play through the following example using quarter notes played with staccato:

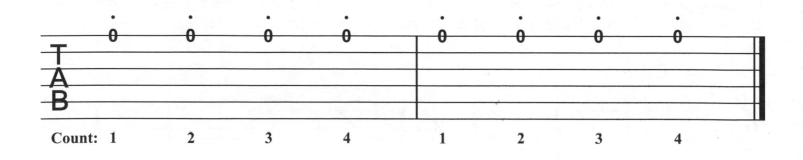

Using Legato with Quarter Notes

Legato is the opposite of staccato. Staccato is short and detached. Legato is connected and flowing; there's no space between the notes, every note flows right into the next one. Play through the following example using legato:

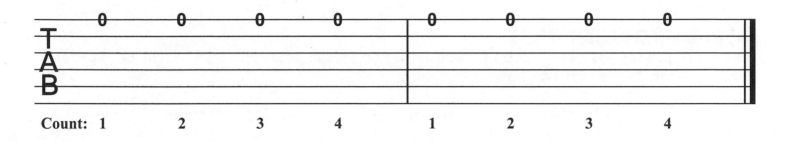

Count: 1   2   3   4   1   2   3   4

Accents

An accent is another articulation in music. Accents are used to notate that a chord or note should be played louder with more emphasis. In music, accents are notated with an arrowhead above a note or a chord. Play through the following example accenting the note on beat 1:

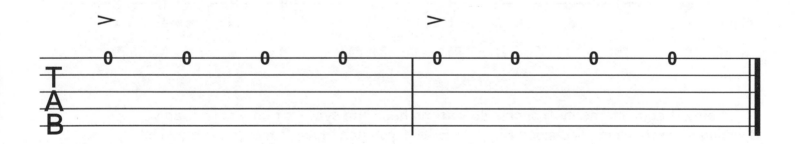

Now play though the same example but this time accent the strum on beat 2.

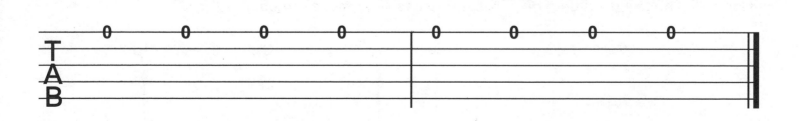

Syncopation

Syncopation by definition is an accent on a normally unaccented beat. Since most people would consider a normal feel for music on the downbeat, most often syncopation is played on the upbeat. When you start hitting notes on an upbeat, it's more unexpected, and it creates a syncopated feel. You are going to learn a couple different strumming patterns that use syncopation.

Strum Pattern # 1

The first pattern is going to be played with the strum pattern down, down-up, up-down. Play through this pattern now:

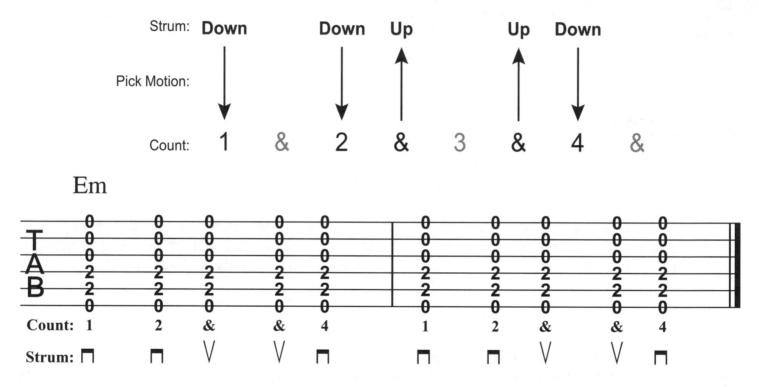

Next play it against the metronome so you can hear the syncopation. Remember you can download a metronome from our Support Site if you don't have a metronome available.

Strum Pattern # 2

The second strum pattern is similar to the first one. Once again, learn the feel of the strum by starting with just muted strums. The strum pattern for this example is down, down-up, up, up. The three up strums in this progression are on the "&'s" after beats 2, 3 and 4. These up strums give the progression a more syncopated feel.

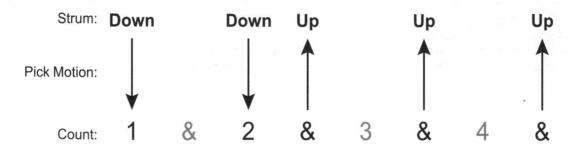

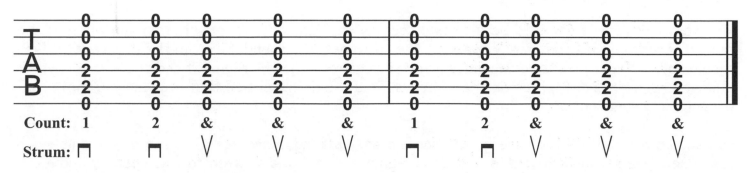

You should begin to experiment with different syncopated rhythms. Use the E and A minor chords to create your own syncopated rhythms.

Musical Styles

In this section, you will learn about different musical styles, or genres of music. I will explain what makes them characteristically different from one another. Many times its what the instruments play or accent within the beat that makes the sound unique. Let's go through and dissect the clichés in the most common genres of modern music.

Rock

Rock is a very common style of music in the United States and around the world. Let's explore a little bit about the characteristics of a rock rhythm. You'll hear on this example that the drums are hitting on the 1, 2, 3, and 4 with the open high hat. Also, on the bass and snare drums, you'll notice that they come in on different beats. The bass drum is on beats 1 and 3 while the snare drum is played on beats 2 and 4.

What you want to hear is the alternation of accents: bass, snare, bass, snare. Notice that a rock beat has more accenting on the down beats. You should also notice that even when the guitar and bass come in, that the accents are still driving hard on the 1, 2, 3 and 4 but also on the "&'s" of beats 3 and 4. So now listen to this example and pay attention to the characteristics we just talked about.

Metal

Many consider Metal to be a form of rock just intensified, and much heavier. You'll notice in the audio example that the bass drum and snare drum are still accenting on beats 1, 2, 3 and 4 with the high hat as in the rock example, but everything is much more "open" giving the track a louder and mushier sound.

However, when it comes to metal music, the guitar takes on a couple of different characteristics that make it really sound metal. You'll notice that when the guitar hits chords, there will be these little palm muted grace notes (or chugging notes) in-between the chords that gives that highly recognizable metal feel.

Country

The next example is going to be a classic country rhythm. Within this rhythm you will notice a few different clichés that really spell out the country music sound. First, in the drum section you should notice that the bass drum plays on all four beats while the high hat and snare drum (which is played with a rim shot) is all on the up beats. It is the drum section that is giving you that country sounding syncopation.

You should also notice that the guitar has a pretty strong characteristic, the guitar employs a bass line while strumming on the chords in eighth notes. Take a listen to this country audio example, and listen to the distinct characteristics that really spell out a country rhythm.

Reggae

Reggae is most known for being the island music of the Caribbean islands. Reggae is a really fun music style to listen to and play. As with the other styles we discussed already, Reggae does have some distinct characteristics you want to be consciously aware of. You'll notice on this audio example that the drummer is still playing with the bass drum on two and four, but on the high hat, the drummer is doing a syncopated shuffle rhythm. You will be learning about the shuffle feel in an upcoming lesson.

The guitar is probably the most characteristic part of reggae music, because the guitar rhythms are most often consistent up strums or a variation of an up beat syncopation. The guitar rhythm tends to be the most intricate part of this music style. Take a listen to the audio example and really pick out the pieces that bring out that "island feel."

Ska

Reggae is compared to ska in the same fashion as rock to metal. Ska seems like it's a more intense, heavier version of that style of music. Ska music is often also faster in tempo; reggae usually has a slower groove and feel.

Ska like reggae is going to have accents on the upbeat, but you will notice in the audio example that the drums have the high hat hitting consistently on the upbeat.

Listen to how the guitar and the bass guitar counter each other's part, which really gives the music the ska feel. The bass guitar is hitting on the down beat of 1, 2, 3 and 4, the guitar is accenting consistent upbeats. This play on the rhythm gives a back and forth motion.

Triplets

Now it is time for you to learn what triplets are and how to play them. Up to this point you have worked on several different note values and everything was subdividing the various beats in half. Now we're going to divide the quarter note into threes. So for every one beat, you are going to play three notes or three strums of a chord. When you divide a beat into three equal parts it is called an eighth note triplet. You count eighth note triplets:

1 – trip – let, 2 – trip – let, 3 – trip – let, 4 – trip – let

Now hold the A minor open chord down that you learned earlier, and strum it in triplets. Really feel that triplet vibe while you strum the chord.

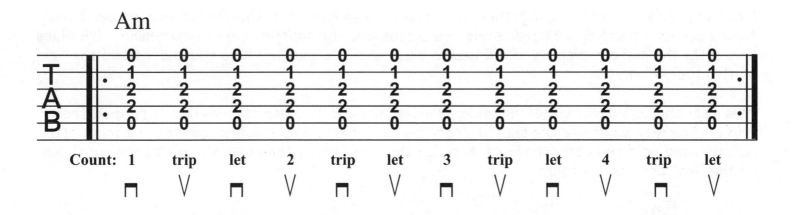

You can, and should, play triplets using all of the chords you know. Start out by alternating back and forth between A and E minor to get that triplet feel going in a chord progression setting.

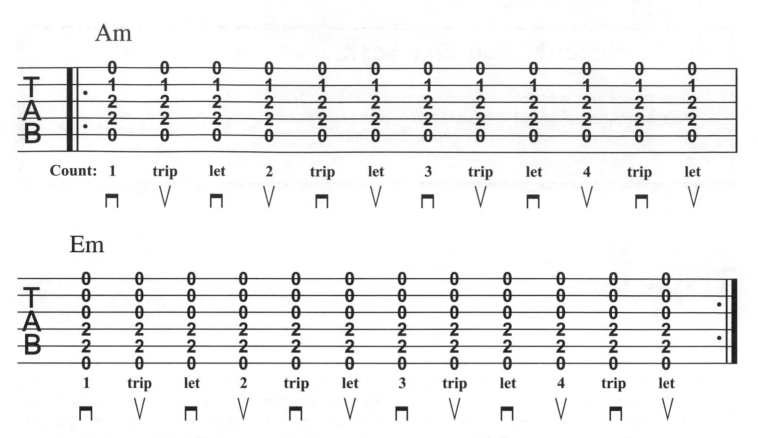

Count: 1   trip   let   2   trip   let   3   trip   let   4   trip   let

Often times you will hear players accent the "1" to emphasize the triplet feel. I encourage you to experiment and most of all have some fun!

The Shuffle or Swing Feel

Once you have the triplets together, it's then time to learn the shuffle (or swing) feel I mentioned earlier when Reggae music style was discussed. The shuffle feel is synonymous with blues music. On the audio example you will hear a blues example that will help you understand the feel of this type of rhythm.

This feel should be learned after understanding triplets because the rhythm is formed from a triplet. The way we derive the shuffle from the triplet is to play the first part of the triplet (the number) and hold the note, or chord, through the "trip" count then play the next note (or chord) on the "let" part of the count.

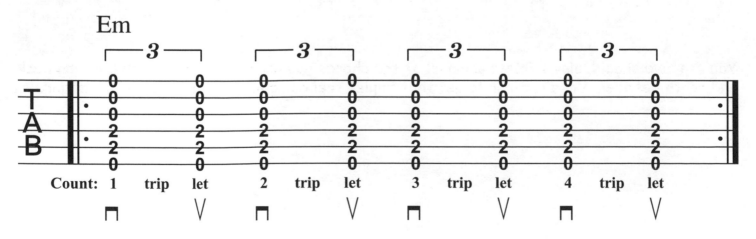

If you are having trouble playing this rhythmic feel, count triplets out loud while clapping the accents on the first and last parts of the count. Once you have the clap steady, stop counting out loud and you will hear the shuffle feel accents. And as I stated, this is well known in the blues genre. Listen to the blues rhythm track to clearly hear the swing feel.

Sixteenth Notes

Up to this point you have learned how to divide beats into two and three equal parts. The last note value and beat subdivision you are going to learn in this program is the sixteenth note, which divides the beat into four equal parts. The eighth notes you learned divided the beat into twos; sixteenth notes are twice as fast as the eighth notes.

To get the feel of the sixteenth notes internalized, mute your strings with your fretting hand and play percussive down and up strums. While strumming count the in sixteenth note timing as follows:

1 e & ah, 2 e & ah, 3 e & ah, 4 e & ah

The number count and the "&" are always down strums whereas the "e'" and "ah" counts are played using up strums.

Count:	1	e	&	ah	2	e	&	ah	3	e	&	ah	4	e	&	ah
Strum:	⊓	V	⊓	V	⊓	V	⊓	V	⊓	V	⊓	V	⊓	V	⊓	V

You should feel and hear there are four subdivisions for every one beat. Now play the sixteenth note feel with the E minor open. It is common for players to accent the "1" when playing this type of feel.

Em

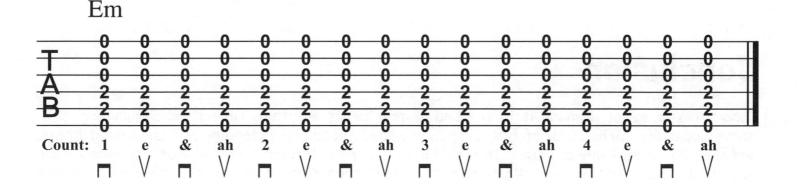

So that's the sixteenth note, and the sixteenth note feel. Practice the examples and get to know and understand this note value.

Time Signatures

The time signature is two numbers on top of each other at the beginning of a piece of sheet music. These numbers tell you how many beats that are in a measure and the type of note receiving one beat. The two most common time signatures are 3/4 timing and 4/4 timing. When you look at a piece of music, before the music notation even starts, you'll see either a four with a line and a four underneath it, or a three with a line and a four underneath it on the staff, that's the indication for 4/4 or 3/4 timing. There's also another symbol for 4/4 timing, a "C", which represents "common time." For now, the number you have to really be most aware of is the top number and that tells you how many beats are in each measure.

In 3/4 timing, there will be three beats in a measure. This means we're counting in threes throughout the piece of music, which is: 1 – 2 – 3 – 1 – 2 – 3 and so on.

In 4/4 timing there is four beats per measure and that is counted: 1 – 2 – 3 – 4 – 1 – 2 – 3 – 4 etc. 3/4 time is used a lot in waltzes, and 4/4 time is used a lot in rock and blues and is the time signature we have been using throughout this program. Learn these two common time signatures and listen to your favorite music and count along to find out what time signature they are using.

4 = Number of beats per measure.
4 = A Quarter note receiving one beat.

4/4	**C**	**3/4**
Indicates four beats per measure.	Four beats per measure. Also known as "common time."	Indicates three beats per measure.

Conclusion

Congratulations, you've made it to the end of the "Beats, Rhythm, Timing and Strumming" program. Hopefully you had a lot of fun, and now you have a good understanding of basic timing, beats, and are strumming away on your guitar. Listen to a lot of different styles of music and make sure you count along with the songs. Remember to go to Rockhousemethod. com to get support for this and all the Rock House programs. Hope to see you on stage one day.

John McCarthy

Crossword Puzzle

Answers are located on page 72

Across

2. Blues is played with this type of feel

5. A small "m" in a chord name indicates this type of chord

6. Which string corresponds to the top line of the tab staff

8. Note that gets two beats

10. Fretting notes by placing one finger flat across more than one string

12. A device that clicks in time at an adjustable speed

13. Note that gets four beats

16. Note that gets half a beat

Down

1. Down-up-down-up picking motion

2. Drum that usually plays on beats 2 and 4

3. Sad sounding chords

4. Note that gets one beat

7. A succession of single notes

9. How many different notes are in a minor pentatonic scale

11. Happy, bright sounding chords

14. Names of the open strings from the 6th string to the 1st string

15. The lowest sounding string

Word Search

Answers are located on page 72

```
I W C C I K Z L O H E J O S O T G S V J V R T L E
N Z K U J Q N O E E M F C H L H V L C B E V W O M
P G B P Q H U T P A T V M L M V H U F R L A H K T
U Z H Y G K T A W D Z H L K D T K P Q I P V M D Y
T T Q C E E N Z G S E Y N G N W E R K D B J V Z Y
J W K B L H G O S T D N E C K T V C X G T P B F U
A Z Y T C L C D V O I Y B W N O G C D E U I O M L
C S X O V U K Y Q C V I V A D U S I F H N C D B A
K C O S A H R T T K U F B Y K Y B L K I E K Y F L
E A D O J X Q Q O P B T B N T E B R A R R U J O Z
Q X H V B H N H D G B L L Y U N C F Q R S P S X G
I G N B Y Q O G N W R Q C U B K P K B W S S N P G
P I C K U P S E L E C T O R S W I T C H J E S R R
F G R D P R S E P C R R E P F O I M G R E L D E T
M P O S I T I O N M A R K E R S L B O Q P U Y B P
W Z C U U E W B Z U C Y R X R P K Q U V B R I H O
T L W O Z E Y V U A Y G C N Y O G S C K Z J F Z K
L I H U F J W G F R E T S J L M V P Z S Y W C T C
I T N J N T J H L T A L F U O I A Z X Y L G Z V X
K C N P S C Q V L T H O D M T V L W F W E F K L R
G Y C R F E V O L U M E A N D T O N E K N O B S P
S L V U R R L V R U R E O C C K O S S B I C G C W
G T J I U X Q K V K F P H A H E U F U D G X O N A
B D N I X A T Z A K K S T R A P B U T T O N K T F
F M Z Q E I D X C Z E C J G Q Q Q E H U V C M Q Y
```

HEADSTOCK	TUNERS	NUT	FRETS
NECK	POSITIONMARKERS	STRAPBUTTON	PICKUPS
BRIDGE	PICKUPSELECTORSWITCH	VOLUMEANDTONEKNOBS	INPUTJACK
BODY			

Changing Strings

Old guitar strings may break or lose their tone and become harder to keep in tune You might feel comfortable at first having a teacher or someone at a music store change your strings for you, but eventually you will need to know how to do it yourself. Changing the strings on a guitar is not as difficult as it may seem and the best way to learn how to do this is by practicing. Guitar strings are fairly inexpensive and you may have to go through a few to get it right the first time you try to restring your guitar. How often you change your strings depends entirely on how much you play your guitar, but if the same strings have been on it for months, it's probably time for a new set.

Most strings attach at the headstock in the same way, however electric and acoustic guitars vary in the way in which the string is attached at the bridge. Before removing the old string from the guitar, examine the way it is attached to the guitar and try to duplicate that with the new string. Acoustic guitars may use removeable bridge pins that fasten the end of the string to the guitar by pushing it into the bridge and securing it there. On some electric guitars, the string may need to be threaded through a hole in the back of the body.

Follow the series of photos below for a basic description of how to change a string. Before trying it yourself, read through the quick tips for beginners on the following

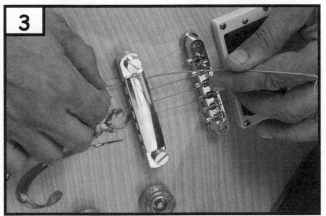
Use a string winder to loosen the string.

Remove the old string from the tuning post.

Pull the old sting through the bridge and discard it.

Remove the new string from the packaging and uncoil it.

Thread the end of the new string through the bridge.

Pull the string along the neck and thread it through the small hole on the tuning post.

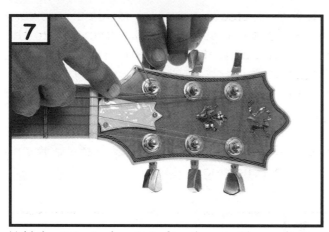

Hold the string in place just after the nut with your finger and tighten up the slack in the string with the machine head.

Carefully tighten the string and tune it to the proper pitch.

You can cut the old string off the guitar but you may want to unwind it instead and save it as a spare in case you break a string later.

Check to make sure you have the correct string in your hand before putting it on the guitar. The strings may be color coded at the end to help you identify them.

Be sure to wind the string around the tuning post in the proper direction (see photos), and leave enough slack to wind the string around the post several times. The string should wind around the post underneath itself to form a nice, neat coil.

Once the extra slack is taken up and the string is taught, tune it very gradually to pitch, being careful not to overtighten and accidentally break the new string. Once the string is on the guitar and tightened up, you can cut the excess string sticking out from the tuning post with a wire cutter. The sharp tail end that is left can be bent downward with the wire cutter to get it out of the way and avoid cutting or stabbing your finger on it.

Check the ends of the string to make sure it is sitting correctly on the proper saddle and space on the nut. New strings will go out of tune very quickly until they are broken in. You can gently massage the new string with your thumbs and fingers once it's on the guitar, slightly stretching the string out and helping to break it in. Then retune the string and repeat this process a few times for each string.

Bonus Chord Section

This bonus section contains additional major and minor open chords. Practice and memorize all of these chords to complete your open chord vocabulary.

F

x x 3 2 1 1

B

x x 2 3 4 1

Cm

3fr

x x 3 4 2 1

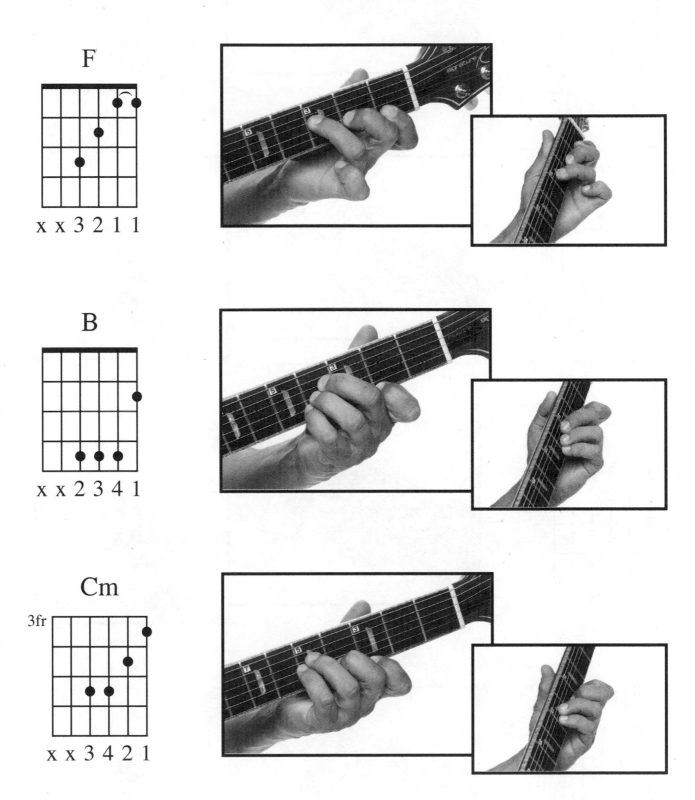

Dm

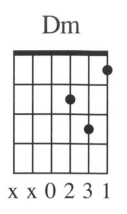

x x 0 2 3 1

Fm

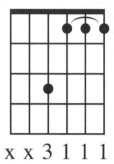

x x 3 1 1 1

Gm

3fr

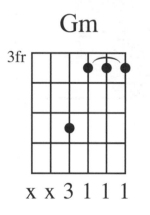

x x 3 1 1 1

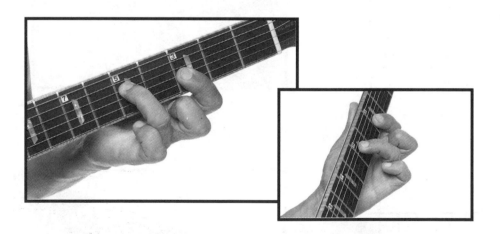

Bm

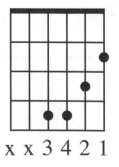

x x 3 4 2 1

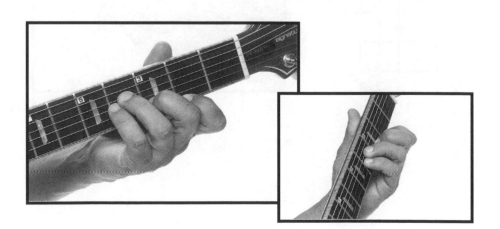

Guitar Accessories

cables

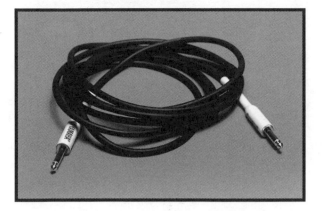

straps

picks

tuner

case

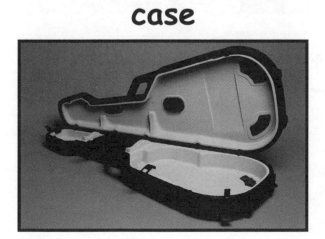

gig bag

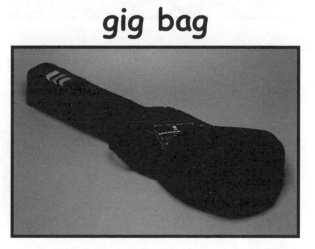

strings

polish

string winder

capo

slide

amplifier

effects

Musical Words

Action - Height of the strings from the fret board to the string itself.

Beat - The regular pulse of music which may be dictated by a metronome, or by the accents in music.

Bridge - The bridge is located on the body of the guitar and transfers sound from the strings to the body of the guitar. This can be held in place by screws or string tension.

Body - The main section of the instrument where the bridge and tailpiece are located.

Chord - The sounding of three or more notes simultaneously.

Fretboard or Fingerboard - The area on top of the neck that you press the string upon to create a note or frequency.

Flat - An accidental symbol placed to the left of a note, indicating that its pitch should be lowered by a half step.

Fret - The metal strips along your fretboard. They come in a variety of sizes. For example, small, medium, medium-jumbo, or jumbo. The size depends on what a player likes best.

Headstock - Top of the instrument where the tuners or machine heads are located.

Interval - The distance between two pitches.

Machine Head - A device to control the tension of the strings. With a slight turn of the machine head, the player can tighten or loosen the tension to raise or lower the pitch of the string until it is in tune.

Melody - A succession of single tones containing rhythm and pitches arranged as a musical shape.

Neck - The middle of the guitar where the strings are stretched over the fretboard.

Nut - Piece of plastic or bone between the headstock and fretboard. Guides the strings from the fretboard to the tuners on the headstock.

Pickguard - Piece of material placed on the body of the guitar to protect it from pick scratches.

Pickup - Device that takes the string vibration that you create and transforms it into an electronic signal. This signal is then sent to the amplifier to boost the sound.

Saddles - Piece on the bridge that holds the string in place.

Scale - A series of notes in ascending or descending order that presents the pitches of a key or mode, beginning and ending on the tonic of that key or mode.

Sharp - An accidental symbol placed to the left of a note, indicating that its pitch should be raised by a half step.

Tempo - The speed of the rhythm of a composition. Tempo is measured according to beats per minute.

Timing - The beat of musical rhythm. The controlled movement of music in time.

Triplet - Three notes of equal length that are to be performed in the duration of two notes of equal length.

```
T
A
B


T
A
B


T
A
B


T
A
B


T
A
B
```

Quiz #1 answers:

1) C
2) A
3) B
4) C
5) C
6) C
7) B

Crossword solution words:
SHUFFLE, SNARE, MINOR, FIRST, QUARTER, HALF, BARRE, METRONOME, WHOLE, EIGHTH, MAJOR, HEADGB, PICKTH, SIXTH

Quiz #2 answers:

1) C
2) B
3) C
4) B
5) A
6) C
7) C

Word search found words: NUT, NECK, BRIDGE, TUNERS, PICKUPS, BODY, PICKUP SELECTOR SWITCH, POSITION MARKERS, FRETS, VOLUME AND TONE KNOBS, STRAP BUTTON, INPUT JACK, HEADSTOCK

MEMBER NUMBER:
GK992253